★ ★

Memorial Day

Lynn Hamilton

Weigl Publishers Inc.

Published by Weigl Publishers Inc.
350 5th Avenue, Suite 3304
New York, NY USA 10118-0069
Web site: www.weigl.com

Library of Congress Cataloging-in-Publication Data

Hamilton, Lynn 1964-
  Memorial Day / Lynn Hamilton.
      p. cm. -- (American holidays)
Summary: Examines the history Memorial Day and describes some of the
ways that this holiday is celebrated.
Includes bibliographical references and index.
  ISBN 1-59036-105-9 (lib. bdg. : alk. paper) — ISBN 1-59036-168-7 (pbk.)
  1. Memorial Day--Juvenile literature.650 [1. Memorial Day. 2.
Holidays.] I. Title. II. American holidays (Mankato, Minn.)
  E642.H23 2004
  394.262--dc21
                                    2003003956

Printed in the United States of America
1 2 3 4 5 6 7 8 9 0 07 06 05 04 03

Project Coordinator Tina Schwartzenberger **Substantive Editor** Heather C. Hudak
Design Terry Paulhus **Layout** Susan Kenyon **Photo Researcher** Barbara Hoffman

Photo Credits
Every reasonable effort has been made to trace ownership and to obtain permission to reprint copyright material. The publishers would be
pleased to have any errors or omissions brought to their attention so that they may be corrected in subsequent printings.

Corbis Corporation: page 21; **Darlene Duprey:** pages 8, 13; **General John A. Logan Museum:** page 10; **John A. Logan College:**
page 11; **Mike Lynaugh:** pages 5, 9T, 9B; **Peter Noyes of Wapakoneta, Ohio:** page 15; **Bryan Pezzi:** page 20; **PhotoSpin, Inc.:**
page 3; **Jim Steinhart of www.planetware.com:** pages 7, 12, 16, 17, 22; **U.S. Army Photo:** page 18.

Contents

Introduction

★ ★

Some people quietly show their respect during private services.

Memorial Day is a national holiday that is observed on the last Monday in May. On this day, the men and women who died serving the United States during times of war are honored. It is also a time to honor the men and women who protect and defend the United States.

On Memorial Day, **veterans**, military personnel, and citizens pay tribute to servicemen and women. Often, special ceremonies are held at **monuments** and cemeteries. Wreaths, flowers, and small U.S. flags are placed on the graves of fallen soldiers. Some people quietly show their respect during private services. They think about the heroes who have served in the past, and present-day soldiers.

Around the world, people place gifts of flowers on graveyards. Flowers represent the beauty and shortness of life.

Civil War

★ ★

The town gathered to help the women decorate the graves.

DID YOU KNOW?

A sign outside Boalsburg, Pennsylvania, reads: "Birthplace of Memorial Day." The custom of decorating soldiers' graves was begun here in October 1864 by Emma Hunter, Sophie Keller, and Elizabeth Meyers.

Between 1861 and 1865, the northern states fought against the southern states in the Civil War. The southern states wanted to become a separate nation. The northern states wanted to keep the country together. **Union** and **Confederate** soldiers fought many battles. About 500,000 soldiers died, and thousands more were wounded.

About twenty-five communities claim to have held the first memorial ceremonies. Boalsburg, Pennsylvania is one of these communities. In 1864, Emma Hunter and Sophie Keller met Elizabeth Meyers. All three women were visiting the graves of family members who had died during the Civil War. They agreed to meet again one year later. They planned to decorate the graves of all the soldiers who died during the Civil War. The following year, the whole town gathered to help them decorate the graves.

Many American cities have Civil War memorials that honor the soldiers who fought in the war. One such memorial is the National Cemetery in Fredericksburg, Virginia.

Remembering the Fallen

★ ★

Henry Welles thought a special day should be set aside each year to honor the fallen soldiers of the Civil War.

Henry Welles lived in Waterloo, New York. He thought a special day should be set aside each year to honor the fallen soldiers of the Civil War. General John B. Murray agreed with Welles's idea. The two men organized a memorial program. On May 5, 1866, businesses closed, and flags flew at **half-staff**. The village was decorated with black streamers and evergreen branches. The people of Waterloo visited nearby cemeteries to place crosses, flowers, and wreaths on the graves.

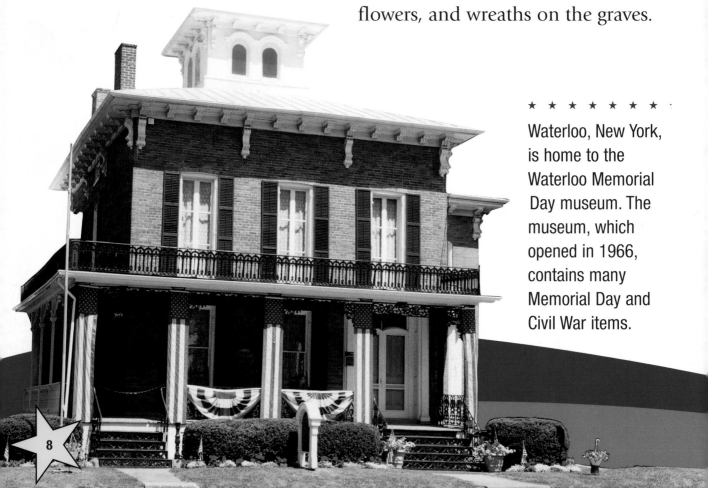

★ ★ ★ ★ ★ ★ ★

Waterloo, New York, is home to the Waterloo Memorial Day museum. The museum, which opened in 1966, contains many Memorial Day and Civil War items.

On Memorial Day 2003, President George W. Bush laid a wreath at the Tomb of the Unknowns during a ceremony in Arlington National Cemetery.

On the Thursday before Memorial Day, soldiers of the 3rd U.S. Infantry place small American flags at each of the more than 260,000 gravestones in Arlington National Cemetery. This has been a tradition since the late 1950s.

Official Order

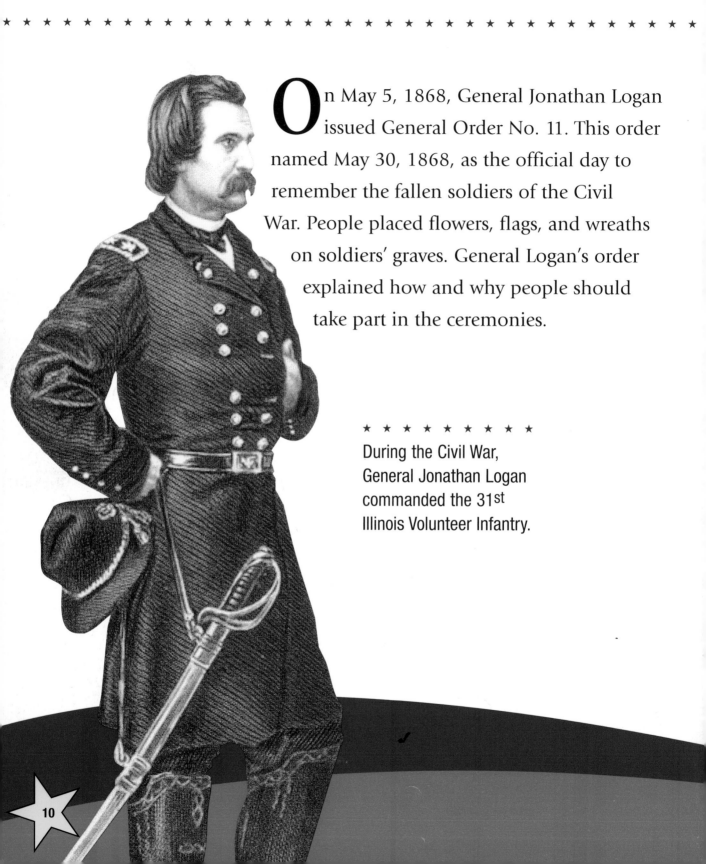

On May 5, 1868, General Jonathan Logan issued General Order No. 11. This order named May 30, 1868, as the official day to remember the fallen soldiers of the Civil War. People placed flowers, flags, and wreaths on soldiers' graves. General Logan's order explained how and why people should take part in the ceremonies.

★ ★ ★ ★ ★ ★ ★ ★

During the Civil War, General Jonathan Logan commanded the 31st Illinois Volunteer Infantry.

General Order No. 11

*The 30th day of May, 1868, is designated for the purpose of strewing with flowers, or otherwise decorating the graves of **comrades** who died in defense of their country and during the late rebellion, and whose bodies now lie in almost every city, village, and hamlet churchyard in the land.*

—General Jonathan Logan

After the Civil War ended, General Logan became a U.S. senator. He also led the Grand Army of the Republic, an organization for war veterans.

Creating the Holiday

★ ★

New York became the first state to name May 30 a legal holiday.

Following General Logan's announcement, ceremonies took place in many communities. About 5,000 people attended the first official ceremony at Arlington National Cemetery in Virginia. Flowers were placed on more than 20,000 Union and Confederate graves.

In 1873, New York became the first state to name May 30 a legal holiday. Soon, many other states did the same. In 1882, May 30 was named Memorial Day. After World War I, people paid tribute to those who died serving in other wars, too.

★ ★ ★ ★ ★ ★ ★ ★ ★

Arlington National Cemetery in Virginia is one of the largest cemeteries in the United States. Most of the people buried in the cemetery were killed during battle.

The U.S. government officially named Waterloo, New York, the "Birthplace of Memorial Day" in 1966. Many other observances had taken place 100 years before Waterloo. Still, Waterloo was the first city to hold a carefully planned ceremony that involved an entire community. In 1971, Memorial Day was made a national holiday. Memorial Day activities were moved to the last Monday in May— making the holiday part of a long weekend.

DID YOU KNOW?

Some southern states continue to hold separate memorial days to honor Confederate soldiers of the Civil War.

During Memorial Day celebrations in Waterloo, New York, the Gettysburg Address is read. Order No. 11, designating Decoration Day, which later became Memorial Day, is also read.

Celebrating Today

★ ★

People visit cemeteries to place flowers, small flags, and wreaths on graves.

On Memorial Day, people across the United States show their respect in many ways. Veterans and servicemen and women participate in parades and ceremonies. People visit cemeteries to place flowers, small flags, and wreaths on graves and monuments. Many ceremonies include memorial prayers, **patriotic** songs, and hymns. "**Taps**" is played, too. Flags are flown at half-staff on government buildings and ships. Flowers are strewn on the water to honor those who died at sea.

Ceremonies are held in Europe to honor the American men and women who died in World War I and World War II. The Overseas Memorial Day Association organizes ceremonies and ensures that flags are placed on the graves of fallen soldiers buried overseas.

DID YOU KNOW?

Since 1990, millions of viewers have watched the National Memorial Day Concert on television.

14

The National Moment of Remembrance program began in 2000. At 3:00 p.m. on Memorial Day, all U.S. citizens should stop for 1 minute of silence, or listen to "Taps."

Americans Celebrate

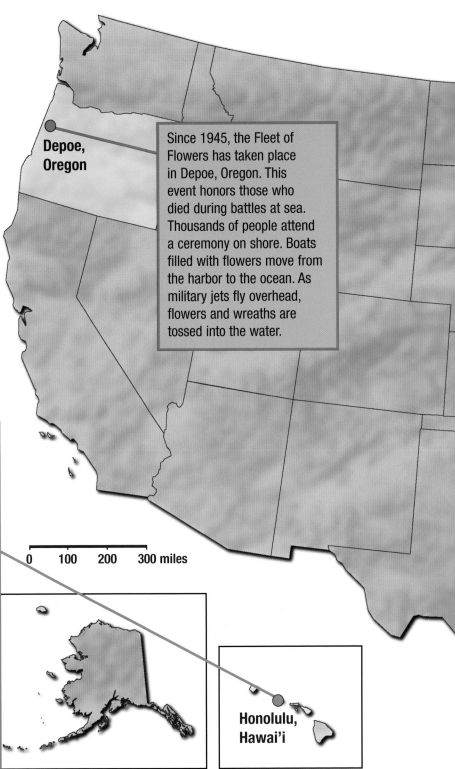

Memorial Day ceremonies are held across the United States each May. Special ceremonies are held to remember the soldiers who were killed serving the country during times of war.

Depoe, Oregon

Since 1945, the Fleet of Flowers has taken place in Depoe, Oregon. This event honors those who died during battles at sea. Thousands of people attend a ceremony on shore. Boats filled with flowers move from the harbor to the ocean. As military jets fly overhead, flowers and wreaths are tossed into the water.

Ceremonies are held each year at the National Memorial Cemetery of the Pacific in Honolulu, Hawai'i. Before the ceremony, Boy Scouts decorate more than 32,000 graves with flags and **leis**. A service is also held at the USS Arizona Memorial to remember those who died in the 1941 attack on Pearl Harbor.

0   100   200   300 miles

Honolulu, Hawai'i

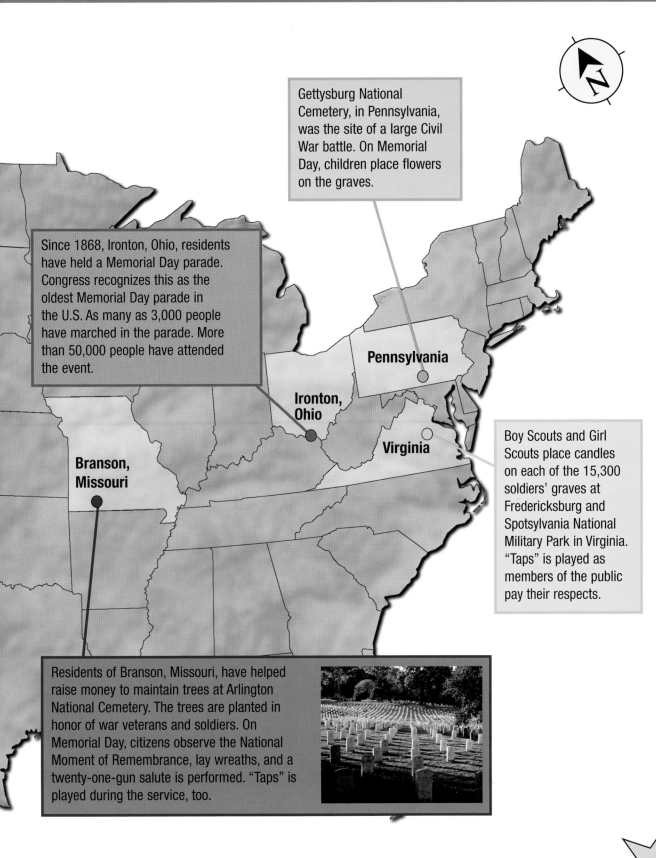

Gettysburg National Cemetery, in Pennsylvania, was the site of a large Civil War battle. On Memorial Day, children place flowers on the graves.

Since 1868, Ironton, Ohio, residents have held a Memorial Day parade. Congress recognizes this as the oldest Memorial Day parade in the U.S. As many as 3,000 people have marched in the parade. More than 50,000 people have attended the event.

Pennsylvania

Ironton, Ohio

Boy Scouts and Girl Scouts place candles on each of the 15,300 soldiers' graves at Fredericksburg and Spotsylvania National Military Park in Virginia. "Taps" is played as members of the public pay their respects.

Virginia

Branson, Missouri

Residents of Branson, Missouri, have helped raise money to maintain trees at Arlington National Cemetery. The trees are planted in honor of war veterans and soldiers. On Memorial Day, citizens observe the National Moment of Remembrance, lay wreaths, and a twenty-one-gun salute is performed. "Taps" is played during the service, too.

Holiday Symbols

Throughout the year, cemeteries, war museums, and monuments remind us of the sacrifices and successes of servicemen and women. Here are some examples of Memorial Day symbols.

Tomb of the Unknowns

The remains of three soldiers have been laid to rest in the Tomb of the Unknowns at Arlington National Cemetery in Virginia. One soldier fought in World War I, one soldier fought in World War II, and one soldier fought in the Korean Conflict. The names of these three men are unknown. Together, they represent the many soldiers who have died while serving their country.

★ ★ ★ ★ ★ ★ ★ ★ ★ ★

On Memorial Day, the U.S. president gives a speech and places a wreath at the Tomb of the Unknowns.

Poppies

In 1915, Moina Michael read "In Flanders Fields." A Canadian military doctor named John McCrae wrote the poem. The poem is about the rows of poppies growing between the graves on a battlefield in Flanders, Belgium. Mrs. Michael wrote her own poem titled "We Shall Keep the Faith." She wrote about wearing poppies to remember fallen soldiers. Today, the poppy is worn as a symbol of remembrance.

Memorials

Memorials honoring fallen soldiers are found across the United States. Many have been built in Washington, D.C. One example is the African American Civil War Memorial. A sculpture named "The Spirit of Freedom" is on display at this memorial. One side of the sculpture is carved with the image of a family as their son leaves to join the war. The other side of the sculpture is carved with the images of three soldiers and a sailor.

Further Research

Many books and Web sites have been developed to explain the history and traditions of Memorial Day. These resources will help you learn more.

Web Sites

To learn about Memorial Day, including the history, memorials, poetry, and speeches, visit:
www.usmemorialday.org

To find out more about the National Moment of Remembrance, visit:
www.remember.gov

Books

Foran, Jill. *American Symbols: Statues and Monuments*. New York: Weigl Publishers Inc., 2003.

Frost, Helen and Gail Saunders-Smith. *Memorial Day*. Minnesota: Pebble Books, 2000.

Crafts and Recipes

Fingerpaint Flag

There are many fun crafts you can create for Memorial Day. For example, you can create a flag using mural paper, and red, white, and blue paint. Take a large piece of mural paper, and paint a blue square in the upper left corner. Then, paint white stars on the blue square. Use your hands to paint red stripes across the rest of the flag. When the mural paper is dry, hang your flag up.

Identify Songs

Use library resources or the Internet to match the songs below to the conflict that it is associated with:

"White Cliffs of Dover"

"Tie a Yellow Ribbon"

"Over There"

"Where Have All the Flowers Gone"

Answers: "White Cliffs of Dover" (WWII); "Tie a Yellow Ribbon" (Desert Storm); "Over There" (WWI); "Where Have All the Flowers Gone" (Vietnam)

Memorial Day Recipe

Memorial Day Salad

Ingredients:

1/2 cup soft cream cheese

1/2 cup mayonnaise

1/2 pound miniature marshmallows, diced

1/2 cup crushed pineapple, well drained

1 cup chopped pecans

dash of salt

1 cup whipping cream, whipped stiff

lettuce

Equipment:

medium-sized bowl

wooden spoon

knife

spatula

large pan

1. Blend the cream cheese and mayonnaise in a medium-sized bowl.
2. Add the marshmallows, pineapple, pecans, and salt.
3. Lightly fold in the cream.
4. Pour into the large pan.
5. Chill overnight.
6. Serve on a bed of lettuce.

Glossary

★ ★ ★ ★ ★ ★ ★ ★ ★ ★ ★ ★ ★ ★ ★ ★ ★

comrades: soldiers and other military members who served in times of war

Confederate: the Southern states of the Civil War

half-staff: a flag lowered about halfway down the flagpole to show respect for the dead

leis: flower necklaces

monuments: objects built in remembrance of a person, place, or event

patriotic: showing love for one's country

"Taps": a military song that is usually played on a trumpet or bugle

Union: the Northern states of the Civil War

veterans: people who have served in the armed forces

Index

★ ★ ★ ★ ★ ★ ★ ★ ★ ★ ★ ★ ★ ★ ★ ★ ★